Enos Prays

written by Tiffany Thomas
illustrated by Nikki Casassa

CFI • An imprint of Cedar Fort, Inc. • Springville, Utah

HARD WORDS:
Enos, prayer, bless

PARENT TIP: Check for understanding. After a few pages, ask the child what has happened in the story so far.

This is Jacob.
Jacob is
Nephi's brother.

Nephi gives the
brass plates to Jacob.

Jacob teaches the people.

Jacob has a son named Enos.

Enos did not want to listen.

Enos goes for a hunt.

Enos says
a prayer.

God blesses Enos and forgives him.

Enos prays for the Nephites
and the Lamanites.

God says He will
bless them.

Enos is happy.

The end.

ISBN 13: 978-1-4621-4337-5

Published by CFI, an imprint of Cedar Fort, Inc. • 2373 W. 700 S., Suite 100, Springville, UT 84663
Distributed by Cedar Fort, Inc., www.cedarfort.com

Cover design and interior layout design by Shawnda T. Craig
Cover design © 2022 Cedar Fort, Inc.
Printed in China • Printed on acid-free paper
10 9 8 7 6 5 4 3 2 1